DISCOVERY PASSAGES

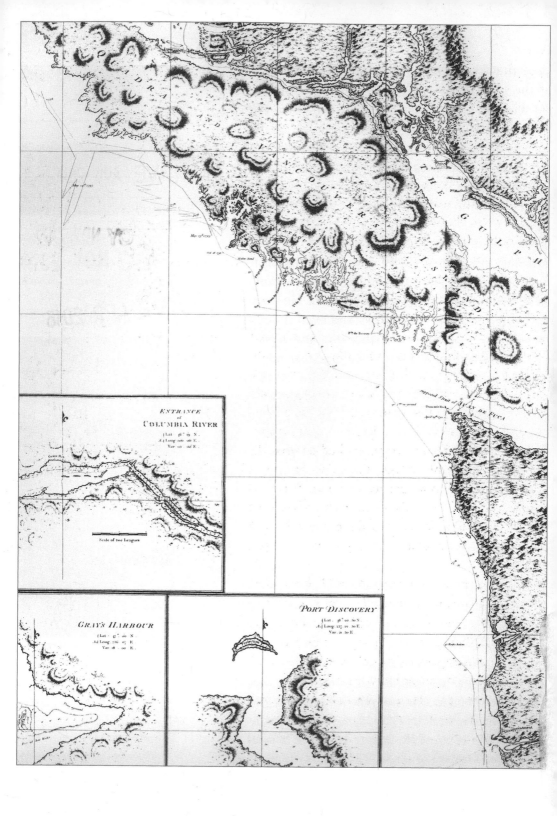

ENTRANCE
of
COLUMBIA RIVER

Scale of two Leagues

GRAY'S HARBOUR

PORT DISCOVERY

Talonbooks

Box 2076, Vancouver, British Columbia, Canada v6b 3s3

www.talonbooks.com

Typeset in Adobe Caslon and printed and bound in Canada.
Printed on 50% post-consumer recycled paper.

First printing: 2011

The publisher gratefully acknowledges the financial support of the Canada Council for the Arts;
the Government of Canada through the Book Publishing Industry Development Program; and
the Province of British Columbia through the British Columbia Arts Council and the Book
Publishing Tax Credit for our publishing activities.

Library and Archives Canada Cataloguing in Publication

Morse, Garry Thomas
Discovery passages / Garry Thomas Morse.

Poems.

ISBN 978-0-88922-660-9   I. Title.

PS8626.O774D57 2011   C811'.6   C2010-907126-3

GARRY THOMAS MORSE

DISCOVERY

PASSAGES

TALONBOOKS

There were so many fish in Discovery Passage then,
you could walk on them!　　　　　　　　*– Harry Assu*

Enter <-

the myth of being *clean*. I too want to write those long clean lines like cedar

planks removed. Tree left,   alive

                                        The way it was always done ...
now
        silviculture

                    Yo, Silvus, say wa?

                                                        The rhetoric
of hidden whistles
                & kelp reeds
                            wafts through
                                        screaming mask

The latest myth
                a dream
            of being
                clean
                    evoking awareness *& sympathy with cedar-
                    plank pink salmon milking a morning farm

swishing
        pale
            white/wash
                    almost
                        so dreamy
                                & clean

'makola

"mom
      are those islands
or only
      shadows?"

Keep Off The Grass

                              Out of the darkness
                    a string
                         of lights
emerge
        garrulous
                    with at least a century
                                    of illumination

    About dark & boardwalk
                              totems
                              loom
                              endowed
                              with death
" *They just*
        let them
                fall
                    a part
        That's their way "

                { thus the deadest are the most in disrepair }

    But
        by
            morning
                    across the planks
                                unpetrified
                                        they
                                        provide
                                        the
                                        light

Fin-de-siècle Renaissance

      Spencer   Hudson   fresh

        water   dam   fish

        cannery   rows

A little ornery
one afternoon
my mother:
      "No way
           you wanna
       know
         what they can ..."

            Dead. Trees. Now
Ecological Park

     We cross the board walk. Water

     bottle. Sole muck. Think I hear

     my heart. *Gwa'wina.* A pair of

     ravens their rhythmic flap of

     wing startles the witches' hair

     moss. An
              obligatory
                      raucous
croak
   followed by
           rather dramatic
                    mimesis
          in reflection
        maybe
    something

heard
      on a passing
           speaker
              another
                  bird
                      then ...

Swamp   Cedars   Silence

all'erta

in

alert

bay

the

absence

of

car

alarms

almost

alarms

Envoy

P'alxala

has come

to the coast. Allow me

to uncork

one or two

chimaeras

even a few

smelt

in my soul-

catcher

Still

a

drop

left

Through the fog

it

wanders

outside

beside

my

self

Mind

how you go

This creature

casts

its own

shadows

hungry for rows of crows along power lines

like

argillite carved, seaborn

charged

with/

out

meaning

Lightless tonight
mind how you carry
home the kerfed box
of watertight objects
& no longer advise
me how to handle

my

own

particulars

Potlatch

You forget
        I am other
                Multitudes   I
don't know
        you want
                the hollowed
                        bottom
    of a
    box
        nor bleeding
              chunks
                  of theatrical
meat
        Perhaps you prefer the smoke
        the tenderizing of flesh amid
        suffused fog

                      But I am yet young-
              blood
                gnawing
                    at corners
              of concrete
regurgitating
        a potluck
            combo
                of uninitiates
      in waiting
          room
              Yup, we are just
                      waiting …

Amid
      apparitions
            &   disappearances

        &
          return

                you forget

                    the Chinook

This too

      is a

    gift

Conversations with Remarkable Elders

Dodie doesn't know her own
people, so to speak, high res.
schools & so on & so forth …

Terms
      like *that chief*
                  tells
   us *bum indians*
             who we
are
    escape
         her lips

Dodie has a sense of humour

The water's good. Real good. Try
the water. They wanted to chlorinate
our water. They took a survey. Our
mayor said bleep bleep. You know
what you can bleepin' do with your
chlorinated water, even a whiff of
the stuff makes me hurl
                signed
                    etc, etc.

Water in Campbell River's the shits

They cut down the fucken trees. Used
to be all green far as the eye could see
What's more they cut 'em all down by
the highway. That's what happened
with the Amazon
             Flash
               floods

Damn Chilean wanted to burn
down the U'mista. Good thing
they got alarms. They gave him

two years for arson. Arson! How
'bout ten? Same's as burnin'
down a church. If he'd burned
down U'mista, I would have

                         strung

                              him up

                                      by

                              the

                              nuts

Trouble is there's no more fish

Like that Findian Island. Sointula
I think Bill Gates' brother or some
guy like that bought the place. I
wish the Nimpkish thought of
that first. Malcolm Island. MS

                        Utopia

The entire time, Dodie
sips her very last swig
of Heineken ever so
 slowly

Drugs. That's our trouble. Too many
pizza joints clearing eighty grand a
year. Five slices a slice. Utopia way
we once got hippy dippy hash cake
a cooking sheet of mushrooms. I
think those elders used to take a
few just now & again

                   Yeah

                    you

                got

                      heroin

Missing? See the pawn shop. People steal
masks & stuff from the elders & pawn it
for coke. Lost a lot of friends. Hope that
crystal meth shit don't make its way up

here. She was a nuisance. He gave her
bad smack. Her

    heart

      exploded

Then they killed the eagles. Took their
claws & feathers. Maybe some Hopi
Buncha dinks. My brother comes home
covered in eagle feathers. You can pick
'em up off the ground. The government
came & took a survey. Said there was
no eagle pop. in Alert Bay. The first
day they start loggin', I tell ya, no
less than thirty-eight eagles are
circling

    I hear

      they always

         return

    to the same nest

Now they take pups & kittens

Trouble is there's no more fish

Dangerous Cargo

The road to Utopia is long ...

Disembarking
at *Sointula*
(Place of Harmony)
I
bump my head
on ferry stairs
& curse rain
& wind

Yeah, it's winter

No books. No local
beer. Beck's *&* Buds
But soup *&* comfort
food are pretty good

A woman on the phone
curses, yet is somehow
driven down on such
a day to unlock the
museum:

If I'd known you was
from Vancouver, I'd
have stayed home

Ahh ... Kavela, an out of
tune piano *&* old dance
hall mural, blue-eyed
Tynjalas, old Edisons,
musical scores, stitching
& fishing gear
a young girl
proudly

brandishing

        hammer

                & sickle

                        opera singers &

                        tailors tossed into

                        the unfarmable

                        amid a live

                                    fog(horn

They didn't let us
talk our own language

but we kids couldn't
wait to be let out &

we'd run under
the bleachers &
gab in Finn

There it is

Nope. Sorry
Dangerous Cargo sailing …

Anyhow, we kill time in the
gift shop. *Sound mind sound*
body. Gabby the owner
reveres the First Nations
& is seeking independence:

Everyone acts like
they're the mayor. All ex-
wives & excavators &
everybody knows what
everybody's doin' …

Hey, the pub is open

Founders, why Matti
Kurikka was editing
the Aika & sent for
A.B. Makela back
in Finland. Why send
Kurikka to buy a cow
he'd come back with
a piano. With Makela
it was the opposite

> *Kurikka was writing on*
> *free love in those days(!)*
> *the early 1900s & they*
> *say he had an eye for*
> *the soprano Makela's*
> *wife. Ended up he*
> *left with half the*
> *colony in tow*
> *left Utopia …*

No more to tell
& the next ferry's
in three hours &
how many pints
in the non-
smoking area?

> *… on the next CSI Sointula …*

Finally. The ferry arrives for a stream
of shivering souls, everyone outside
since the passenger waiting area is
fogged up with two really fat joints
the girl sick out of her wits & the
other little puke coaxing her to

escape from *Utopia*

Contra/punctus

             Even in my dreams   I
antagonize
                  Name, rank, & kin
                                  Sure

But
    curmudgeonly
                    around
                        Cape Mudge
                                  I hang
          through
                    smoke   hole

)eyes
                                bulging
                  my groan
                            abominable
with scarcely
              a sacred
                        bone
                            in wing
                                    or beak
            picking through past
refuse
            clawing at shreds
                            hassling
                                    cannibal
                                            spirit
                        on the roof
                                      offering
dead/
      wood
          down dim
      grim alley-
          ways
                all the while firing freely on the healers

& fading

        through the smoke

                         again

On the
     contrary

       You never saw me

Tongue

                   is all about the art
of unlearning
           Suddenly forget
my
    self
        a crowd
            of ðorns
                in my mouth

Vowels shift. Are shifty
Consonants conspire
            Even the student
                      loan-
words
      reimburse me
            slightly:
                How you like
                them abals?

A sudden search, a
whisper in the dark
of nothings adrift:

           Xwalkw, k'ikw, kw'ikw, xwak'wana

& a little bit
        of history
            slows
               to a glottal
                  stop

Copper

              fiercely
              beaten
          with crest
           soundly
           incised

misplaced
         in a deep pocket

                  of history
                      (ἰστορία -
                            means of inquiry
                     a search …

Fat & heavy
          remember
               the worth
                   the bond
                       the pound
of flesh
        bitten out of face-
                 biting societies
                       Then
                         recall

        operatic
        challenge
        to *break*
        copper
             to save
                 face
                 or face shame
                       Copper
bear
     witness
        to every name
              with your animal
                    prints
             your faintest
                trace

of lineage
        & smelted
                memory

                        Present
                           The
                              Document

Petroglyph
Quadra Island, British Columbia

Photo: Catherine Gilbert.

No Comment

The Kwahkewlth
Agency comprehends
25 bands and 2,264
Indians, who are
the most
depraved
and
uncivilized
in the
Province

> *… t]he ruinous Potlache feast is constantly held by them*

John A. Macdonald

Yesterday
today
violating
section
holding
mourning
ceremonies
singing
mourning
songs
receiving
gifts

surviving
relatives
have not
interfered

Wm. M. Halliday, *Indian Agent*
June 13, 1913

In
addition
band
habit
giving
potlatch
each birth
marriage
or death

warn you

the habit
stopped

must be
enforced
those who
break

punished

Wm. M. Halliday, *Indian Agent*
September 1, 1914

puzzel us
settle these matter
up with Mr Ditch
burn who said he
like the potlatch
& dance
at the time
he come to
Cape Mudge

"Charlie Homishernes"
"Tom Lakieza" (Indian)
Quathiaski Cove, B.C.
September 21, 1914

you know
yourself
cost us
& this
copper
just like
big bank

We
keep on
Potlatch
until the
last day

If you
keep on
stop us, you
come round
to kill us

from Tsa wa da i nuk
Kingcome River, B.C.
Sept 21, 1914

whole
social
system

if
falls
into water
gives

if
falls
down
on the street
gives

disgrace
marries
gives

death
gives

birth
gives away
and so on

approaches
socialism
desire
Indian
give away

Wm. M. Halliday, *Indian Agent*
March 3, 1915

gatherings
lose waste
substance
contract
diseases
unfit
British
Subjects
proper sense
prosecute
general
public
Judges
did not
understand
I realize the evil
of the Potlatch
position
IDLERS ACT
framed
good work

white fishermen
on strike
intimidated
the Indians
instances
fish they
would be
drowned
another
strike
look after
my Indians

Wm. M. Halliday, *Indian Agent*
May 29, 1918

Last
spring
arranging
a feast of
oolichan
grease
some
time
about
Xmas
advise
you
sell
grease
give
away
against
the act
persist
no choice
compelled
prosecuted
govern
accordingly

Wm. M. Halliday, *Indian Agent*
Nov. 20, 1918

respect

fully send
a good
straight man
see what a
potlatch is

white friends
giving presents

why can we not
do the same?

white friends
give feasts

why can we not
do the same?

They dance
why should
we not be
allowed
to dance
also

Kwakewlth, Mamalilikulla,
Nimpkish, Tanakteuk, Matilpi,
Tsawataineuk, and the Nuwitti Bands
Dec. 20, 1918

appreciate
Indian chiefs
came to Ottawa
privately

cool
reception
from Scott

fully
appreciate
your petty
troubles

to Mrs. Halliday
and the little girl, I am,

H.S. Clements
House of Commons, Ottawa
May 16, 1919

private
confidential
appreciate

Privately
Scott
Ditch
burn's
report

been so busy
not bothered

quite
appreciate

H.S. Clements
House of Commons, Ottawa
June 4, 1919

The
Department
pleased to
receive
any
representations
Indians
desire

Duncan C. Scott, *Deputy*
Superintendent General, Ottawa
Feb 6, 1920

sentenced
two months

potlatching
going on
bad as
ever
without
foundation

pig sty
reserves

Alert
Bay
Reserve
the cleanest

the cleanest

Sergt. D. Angermann
Jan. 28, 1921

big potlatch
reported at
Christmas

investigated
by police

the court
any way
biased

Wm. M. Halliday, *Indian Agent*
Dec. 21, 1921

Chief Billy
just in asked
his son Dan
get back soon
not lose time
work twelve
days forty
wife children
plead guilty
paraphe[r]nalia
sentence early
His
dance
masks etc
have been
turned in
however
the main
thing

I have a big
wedding in
Campbell
River

Thanking
interest
welfare
people
speedy
conclusion

R.C. Scott
Crosby Marine Mission
April 5, 1922

To Duncan C. Scott,
Deputy Superintendent Indian Aff[ai]rs

too
much
credit
Anger
mann
Royal
Canadian
Mounted
Police
worked
very
hard
indefatigable
efforts
absolute
suppression
this
crying
evil
the
potlatch

Indians
now
inspired

whole
some
fear
of
the
law

with
regard
material
surrendered
piled
in my
wood
shed
present
time

300
cubic
feet
masks
head
dresses
other
pot
latch
gear
yet time
tabulate
every
thing
valuable
very
rare
good
prices
museum
purposes
acquaint
museums
material
valuable

preserve
it
in
our
own
country
with
regard
coppers
surrendered

unique
collection
obtained
owners
price
paid

$245.00 to
$10,500.00

sacrifice
surrender

exhibit

Your Obedient Servant,
Wm. M. Halliday, *Indian Agent*
April 10, 1922

With
regard
large
amount
potlatch
material
collected
tabulate

beg to say
shall draw
attention
museum
authorities

glad
express
appreciation
good
work

you
and
Anger
mann

J.D. McLean, *Acting Deputy Supt. General*
April 19, 1922

47

Potlatch
paraphernalia
surrendered
by
Kwawkewlth
Indians

kindly
securely
boxed
up and
shipped
Anthropological
Division
Department
of
Mine
s   Victoria
Museum
Ottawa
Canada

compensation
attention

Government
cannot
hope
value
paid
in
whole
in
part

Duncan Scott, *Deputy Supt. General*
June 6, 1922

considerable
crating

considerable
amount
labor
involved
segregating
exhibit

fair
amount
set on
paraphernalia

belonging

Wm. M. Halliday, *Indian Agent*
June 23, 1922

few
lines
call all
Indians
shake
hands
money
thank
sympathy
kindness

recent sad
bereavement
loss our
beloved
daughter

permission
no wrong
in it
look up
10 chapter
St. Mark
ver. 17–21

see I do
right

Yours very truly,
Dan Quatell (*Indian*)
July 14, 1922

P.S. *I did not want to ask our agent*
because I know that he won't do it

D.Q.

Department
sympathizes

bereavement
not possible

sanction
violation

Section
149

Indian
Act

J.D. McLean, *Acting Deputy Supt. General*
July 20, 1922

To W.E. Ditchburn

do not like make
complaint against
other agent but
Mr. Matthews
Provincial Constable
told me
Provincial Constable
Broughton
I believe
told Mr. Matthews
he had personally
taken up
potlatch
with Mr. Fougner
asked him if
he wished
prosecution
follow the
potlatch
Act the
reply was

"Let it slip
it is not
worth
taking
any
steps."

and man
on a jury
Vancouver
inferred in
the letter

that the
"pooh-bah"
of Alert Bay
was taking up
this matter to
the detriment
of the Indians

Wm. M. Halliday, *Indian Agent*
June 29, 1922

To W.E. Ditchburn

painful

believe
there is
a public
official
so minded

deliberate
falsehood

an official
seeks favour
making false
statements

brings
official
disfavour?

Your Obedient servant,
(Signed) Iver Fougner, *Indian Agent*
Bella Coola – August 11, 1922

disposal of
paraphernalia
surrendered by
Indians not yet
time
property
crated
packed
ready

Yesterday
Mr. G.W.
H[e]ye
representing
New York
museum
wanted
to buy
stuff
prices
good
sold
$291.00
endorsed to
Department of
Indian Affairs
aware
exceeded
disposal
but object
money for
Indians
action
fully justified
absolutely certain

Wm. M. Halliday, *Indian Agent*

Department
at
a
loss

understand
disposing
without
authority

should
have
remained
in a
Canadian
museum

not
sufficient

unwarranted
action

presume
however

articles
are now
beyond
recall

J.D. McLean, *Asst., Deputy & Sec.,*
Sept. 20, 1922

enclosing
shipping
bill 17

parcels

Indian
Curios
left
on
S.S.
"Celtic"

sent by
C.P.R.
marked
Dr. E.
Sapir
Victoria
Museum
Ottawa

Wm. M. Halliday, *Indian Agent*
Sept. 27, 1922

genuine
Xmas
party

genuine
Xmas
merry
making

none
of the
old time
festivities

young folks
dancing in
ac[c]redited
White
fashion

Fox–
Trotting
Waltzing
etc. etc.

R.C. Scott
Crosby Marine Mission
December 26, 1922

The Secretary, Dept. of Indian Affairs

rank
injustice
quashing
convictions
appeal
against
quashing
convictions

all
my
work
the
last
ten
years
suppression
of
the
potlatch
nullified
by
this
action
of
the
court

The
Indians
in
ignorance
will
take
to
mean

the
courts
are
upholding
them

for
this
reason
ask
returned
to
O[a]kalla

I
will
say
convictions
for
potlatching
do
not
meet
with
favorable
comment
by
the
general
public

regret[t]able
part
the
whole
thing
all
the
work
done
with

regard
to
potlatch
nullified

have
to
be
done
all
over
again

futility

custom
detrimental

give
it
up

Wm. M. Halliday, *Indian Agent*
April 14, 1923

The Indian Picture Opera*

(now in Stereo-Opticon and featuring Magic Lantern technology)

From the people who brought you *The Edward Curtis Project* ...

Creative Non-Fiction Escapades of the Kwakiutl [sic]

> "Nah."
> "Huh?"
> "What's with the title?"
> "What's wrong with it?"
> "Too thinky. We need some damned thing to capture the
> imagination of the public!"
> "If you have a better idea ..."
> "Sho. Sho. How about ..."

In the Land of the Head Hunters
(based on a true people)

*a glimpse of the primitive Americans as they lived in the Stone Age
and as they were still living when the hardy explorers Perez, Heceta
Quadra, Cook, Meares, and Vancouver touched the shores of the
Pacific between 1774 and 1791 ...*

> "That ain't right."
> "Huh?"
> "Don't mean to split hairs but that was Coast Salish
> territory till the Kwakwaka'wakw kicked 'em out. Took
> over the whole island, the way I hears it."

*The native dwellers in this land are seagoing people whose character seems
in harmony with their gloomy, forbidding homeland. In warfare they are head-
hunters with small regard for life, and ceremonial cannibalism is not unknown
Their mentality is to the Caucasian difficult of comprehension; their conclusions
are seemingly inverse ...*

---

* In 1911, to promote book sales, Edward Curtis created a travelling slide show, *The Indian Picture Opera*.

Meet Motana. He's the son of a great-chief in pre-Contact times. But he's about to find out that sometimes … to forfend the anger of the spirits … you end up in some … pretty strange places … like fast asleep on the Island of the Dead …

> AGAIN I turn my thoughts from maids, from food, from worldly things, and think of songs and magic. To yonder gloomy Island of the Dead my canoe will take me. Through the tangled, gruesome jungle I will make my way. In tree above me, in cave beside me, in box, canoe, and bundle, are the Dead!

Disclaimer: some aspects of *In the Land of the Head Hunters* do not accurately depict the essence of Kwakwaka'wakw life or culture including the long-abandoned practices of sorcery, finagling human remains, and the whole head hunting thing. In some cases, artifacts situation and setting may be from neighbouring tribes. Look for the symbol of authenticity. In some cases several Jeep Grand Cherokees were removed from the original film footage

Success or failure in every effort is dependent on the spirits, good or evil. It matters not whether it be the taking of small fish, the capture of the largest whale, or success in war, spirits govern all

> "Trouble is they don't whale either."
> "Don't whale?"
> "They don't whale."
> "Why, I've never heard of not whaling!"
> "Scratch the whale."
> "No, we absolutely must have a whale!"
> "How we gonna come up with a whale at this hour?"
> "We'll rent one!"
> "Rent a whale?"
> "Rent a whale!"

We'll rent a whale / we'll rent a whale / for it will be / a whale of a tale
We'll give the people what they want / we'll give the people what they love
Because everyone wants a whale / yes you and me and they and she and
Everyone wants a whale
There's a good chap / There's a good fellow
No need to bellow / No need to be thick

Just lie back and think of Moby Dick
Because everyone wants a whale / yes you and me and they and she and
Everyone everyone everyone I mean everyone wants a whaaaaaaaaaaaaale

[Furious applause. Scene shifts to Motana in mid-soliloquy]

Me miserable!
Left upon lower plains of the uncanny
Shadow World. Here was a stream
Beautiful, murmuring, soothing, lulling
Mingling with ghostly trees, swaying
Drooping heavy with owls
The Spirits of the Dead

Away with this hour of dreams! What strange thoughts
Oppress me? The spirits have been close, and supernatural
Power is mine, I know. My heart should sing with joy. Yet
Some vague voice warns me of disaster

I touch my throat!
Ha!
My necklace stolen!
Locks of my hair have been cut!

[Cue a lone figure writhing in the background. It is one of
the more attractive Gwa'wina Dancers. She is going places]

One by one the stars come blinking
Above me stretches the flickering
Milky
Way from sea to sea
The sea itself is molten stars
Leaving trails of liquid fire
Close by, with spout and plunge
Sports the great blue whale
Seals lift their glistening dog-
Like heads from phosphorescent
Sea. A school of porpoise!

My father will tell you that, as is the way of the
Kwakiutl [sic], he sent me on this journey, to fast

To pray, to talk with the Spirit Ones of the Earth
Of the Sky, of the Air and the World of the Dead
All these laws have I followed, and have found
Much knowledge

"All right. Time for a teaching moment. How many of my brothers and sisters
are in the house? Yeah? I can't hear you! But Kwakiutl is totes a misnomer.
That is like Juan de F*cked up! You know you just know when you are in the
presence of the Kwakwaka'wakw. Yeah! Kwakwaka'wakw, that's right. Now say
it with me! Kwakwaka'wakw! Yeah, you in the front! Kwakwaka'wakw. Now,
those people asleep in the back. Kwakwaka'wakw. And one more time for the
Metropolitan Museum in Mannahatta! Kwakwaka'wakw!"

"Meh. Needs something."
"Oh yeah, wiseguy?"
"How about a love interest?"
"Love, sho. Sho."
"And she has to marry a Sorcerer."
"Sorcerer, got it."
"'Cept he's all old and ugly and gross."
"Awful and fugly, got it."

An epic story of love and war set before European contact

(and introducing Margaret Frank as
    the lovely Princess Ohmygollees)

Ho, ye! Ho, ye!

Four moons ago the canoes of Yadayadayada
Came to beg the daughter of our proud chief

Ho, ye! Ho, ye!

Great is the chief who thus came begging
For our richest gift, and vast the wealth of
Presents he brought to prove his pride
And tribal standing. Did I mention he
Was well to do?

Ho, ye! Ho, ye!
Wives of every house, prepare much

Food for great must be the wedding
Feast

[Edward Curtis stands in hip-waders at the tideline
cranking his camera on a tripod. A woman at the stern
is dancing and singing. The canoe hits a rock and the
women topple over. Everyone bursts into laughter
except for Edward Curtis, who rips the film out of his
camera and tosses it aside]

"This is a serious film. I don't want *my* Indians
    to laugh."

Disclaimer: some aspects of the film do accurately portray
Kwakwaka'wakw rituals that were, at the time, prohibited by
Canada's potlatch law, enacted in 1884 and not rescinded until
1951, although no potlatches were harmed during the making
of *In the Land of the Head Hunters*

Hi, yu, hi, yu
Here and there
Here and there
This hand, that hand
Right hand, left hand
Left hand, right hand
Which hand

Look! Look!
The crawling things are men
The monster bird must truly be a canoe
Of the spirit world, for men could not dream
Of one so great. It roars with thunder!
Its mouth is belching smoke!
Its wings are falling!
Now it only drifts up on the water
Are the men upon its back
Flesh or spirits?

"So what's our market for this picture?"
"I'm thinking this could be really big!"
"Head Hunters in the Park!"

"Bigger …"
"Lavish Off-Broadway Musical!"
"Bigger …"
"Genocide museum?"
"I like the way you think!"

Hoi ho!

If we are to die, let us die as Kwakiutl
Should

Hoi ho!

"What'dya say? Kwakwaka'wakw! I can't hear you. Kwakwaka'wakw! Now beat
your paddles! Kwakwaka'wakw! Now bang your drum! Kwakwaka'wakw!"

Man to his paddle, and now
To fight these foaming
Rapids

Hoi ho! Hoi ho! Hoi hoooo!

"So, how does it end?"
"You know how it ends."
"With the river and the dying?"
"Yeah."
"How about Motana suddenly realizes he's always loved Naida …"
"… and hurries in his canoe to tell her …"
"… and at the last second stops her from leaving …"
"… and they paddle off into the sunset …"
"Rom coms are very hot right now."

You be strong, you survive. You
Stay alive no matter what occurs
I will find you …

In the Land of the Head Hunters [in 3-D]

You will sooooo lose your head

Gakhula

Most often intruder. Pale-faced intruder
wherever I go. I walk into the museum
without the word (*humu'wilas*) to a lack

amusement like the queen I understand
& writing lost names in the guest book
is similar. Forgo that native manner of

Hamlet or the sluggish drag of Orestes
by Furies. I was told I could touch. An
oral tale. A myth. Within the interview

I seek under glass, I locate the gift shop
on my way out & instead of bracelets
the Danish women covet I will rather

haggle over a language
                                still
                                        breathing
breathless
              still
                        reading
        the receipt

                        baxwam NO TAX

Bak'was

                flashes
                        his hooked
                                nose
    & feeds
        upon
                rotted wood
            grubs
                    spiders
        & stray
            creeps
                    of crawlies
                            Beware
    of Bak'was
                Chief of Ghosts
                        Take not
    the dried salmon
                of Bak'was
                        It is mere
                    dead/
                        wood
                                You
    may become ghost
                A ghost

                            On the brighter side, season-wise
                            Bak'was has a real hankering for
                            cockles. He loves to sojourn in
                            the intertidal zone *&* gather his
                            cockles at leisure. By all means
                            allow him to collect his cockles

        Bak'was is in fact
    tiny
            green
                    & hairy
                            & loves to hunt clams

But take no

photographs
    of this keeper
        of drowned
           souls

          Bak'was
     is
      rather shy

Dzunuk'wa

               devours village
                              children
& is not
          fussy
                    on motorcycle
                                   engines
                         car alarms
                                   or powerboat
                                                 motors
          On ladles
                    dishes, sticks
                              & daggers
dozy
     she sWiShEs
                    the water of life
                                        between
                                        pendulous
                                        breasts
& the wild
          urchins
                    look pretty
                                   interested
                    in getting
                              eaten
          but
          a sprinkle
          brings them
          back to life
                         I
                              assume
nothing
          not her pursed lips
                              howling
               uu
                    huu
                    uu

71

                    nor her obscene
image
        that beckons
                    from the green
                            with a
haunting
        sWiSh/sWiSh
                right through
                                my
                                    dream
                catcher (

Wolf Dish

Samson the great white
husky
up
goes running   &
down

the unpedestrian whale-road
singing
for supper

'wat'si
the dog who dreamed
he was
a wolf
& is
somewhat undomestic

On Cormorant Is
cormorants
look on
while Samson
keen-eyed
& fetter/
less
is delivered
a lovely
meaty
leftover

"Cormorant,"
laughs the man
at the lodge
"Looks
more like
a dog bone to me!"
& Samson continues
to bay
for seconds

to howl through
the rain
while dark myths
beat obsidian wings
against the wind
plotting
perpetuity

Cloak

In a glance
          I half-
     unfasten the black
               button blanket
about her
shoulders
          Snapper-red
          buttons
               tenderly
                    decorate
          her back
                    unsnapped
     Her cloak
   leaps across
   the heated
rocks
     flaps
          impishly in the Nimpkish
                              wind
                         Finally
                              she
                         unwinds
               her long dark locks
& offers salal lips
               & the promise
of a purple conch
          A look
               in her eyes
                    & the sensation
          along her cold thighs
                    all candlefish
                              & slippery
                         light

Yet in the fire
          & sand & sweat & heat
                    the tree of life
                              excitedly
                                   stretches
                                        its limbs

Petroglyph
Quadra Island, British Columbia

Photo: Catherine Gilbert.

Petrograph

hard	live
love	hard
live	love

love	love
hard	live
live	hard

live	hard
love	live
hard	love

Un
    buckled Wamp
        um

mmmm
      beads
           of
               mnemonic
roll
   down
        my brow/
beaten
     feeling
         a memory
of *brown*
       in my cousin's
             mouth
    that firm look
          of defeat
then
     within
        this passing
           glisten
a mischievous
       gleam
         &
        (a)
           wanton
             >flash<
   of wet
      para/
        graphs

Hot Blooded: A Love Poem
for Duncan Campbell Scott

Others don't like the way he's always busy writing
stuff in the notebook he carries. Him,
he calls it poetry
and says it will make us who are doomed
live forever.
          – Armand Garnet Ruffo

Hurry up. Take 'em off
right now I don't wanna
wait I don't got no self-
control whatever O who
can stand it a second
longer this madness
to your Methodizin'
your pockets are
so full of poems
& desire so full
of somethin', so

take off your pants

Or should I say britches
you sexy son of a birch?
Wait. Maybe there's still
time to clear your ivory
throat of sacred words
stomach lurchin' on
larch, rather takin'
a very self-
                satisfyin'
        crap
between
        legions of cedars

  & tamaracks   to
          finally answer
    the call –
        ahhh …
           of nature!

Why, Duncan Campbell Scott
why what can you be thinkin'
tonight, how cling to umbilical
roots of Mother Earth, how
plot biblical expansions deep
in the backward as you muse
on an exposed tit of Titian
& undulations of Umbria
through a chalky layer of
Giotto's to keep out the
elements, frescoes where
St. Francis washes your
dishes, although you sure
made some images, *yours*
your Onondaga Madonna
of a weird & waning race
cradles wizened face to
Lake Nipigon & suckles
even while the Angel of
Death dangles through
the roof & annunciates:

        cranial
         size *does*
        matter

Why, Duncan, you look a little
bushed. Can it be you so bash-
full in front of a half-breed
boy, let alone the full-blooded
girls by half-measures abducted
first fondled then beaten by the
Word then redly let into your
sanctimonious bowl – albeit
you may have paid for it   O
yeah, she was free of *trap &*

paddle all right, portaged
across the vast expanse of
waning moons & muddy
races & dumped into a
residential trap, then
paddled all night

but I contradict myself

Throb-throb-throb-throb;-
Is this throbbing a sound
Or an ache in the air?
Or the confused pound
of a pretty officious penis
dripping Duncan Hancock
& welling up the nearest
place-name with double-
speak. Why, who could tell
what was throbbing behind
your pines? Surely not a
confiscated drum, only a
lock turning in Oakalla
& your cabinet, aside
from the swift remote
unbuckling of a belt

    O Da-ha-wen-non-tye

                my sealed utter of air

                            drifting off

                  wafting by

foppish flapper of propaganda
proud plucker of inviolate pride
excuse my speech, I must have
spit out your honeyed bread
& rich wine a century ago
so last week, you know

So put on some music
& let's get down to
business

Why, the 'wam
is stiflin' tonight. I must
want it real bad all savage
& animalistic & I bet you
like it rough, Mister
        Deputy Superintendent
        General, or Secret
        Indian Agent Man …
                        Don't make me
                        take 'em off
                        for you!

& then

        when you awaken,
        totally blown by
        tenebrous sunset

        I am not here my
        beloved
                only a
                few notes upon
                odorous dresser

                Compensation
                Enough
                        Sorry
                                the thrill is gone
                                the spell is spent
                        & sincerely
                        I just wanted
                        my shit back

                        Your obedient servant, etc

                        The Poet

Gagisamak

she
alone

has the
power

to
sting
me

Billy Assu and family inside his Big House, Cape
Mudge, c. 1918. *left to right*: Thomas Assu, Frank
Assu, Billy Assu, Susan Quocksister (seated with
infant Herman), Lucy Chickite and son Edward,
Harry Assu.

*Image D-04578 courtesy of the Assu family and
the Royal BC Museum, BC Archives.*

Hamat'sa

The Kwakiutl youth aspires
to become hamatsa, the elite,
his patron Baxbakualanuxsiwae,
in a word, he-who-may-eat-human-flesh,
four pieces at a time,
to swallow without chewing,
then disgorge with swallowed sea water.

– George Bowering

I

I am the Kwakiutl youth
with ambition I 'spire
with *nwaluk* I talk
to spirits of long
dead winter
      Van
Morrison why dont you
meet me under that Indian
Summer under (a) pavement
of cement
    leaves

IloveyouIconsumeyouIloveyouIeatyou

to pieces Is 4 per day longer
than most operas entr'acte
is daily supplement
      enough

I start on the East
Indian woman in Walmart
dumping bars of Toblerone
into a shady perambulator

I tighten my mask
                of store dick &
corner her
                outside the strip mall

                                    Chomp(fire) Chomp(fire)
                        Chomp(fire) Chomp(fire)

        Rush home & masticate
        this masala mix & spit
        like a sommelier into
        wilted wolfeared Glas

        My pockets stuffed
        with stolen fire
        with sun & moon
        & impulse rag
        & candied good

II

I am the Kwakiutl youth
I walk repo'd beaches
& hunt killer whales
with muddied looks

while a creature creeps
backward into pink
conches
                I hear its words crunch
beneath my Oxfords
later crackle
                with static eyes
        a gesture to
                        what matter
        I know her
at 1st
        & Vine
                    her deconstructed
clothes of kelp

her phallic watch fob
              a floating bulb
        inside my head

On the sly I am already
eating her at the *potlâche*
behind the scenes
                    clearing her snatches
shaving her conditional wood of
ifs on Yew
          munching on omnivorous brush

                              Chomp(cedar) Chomp(cedar)
                              Chomp(cedar) Chomp(cedar)

Our treaty on the back
of a damp serviette said
nothing about having you
for break/fast

                    I wear the face of Bak'was
                    & sink my gestalt teeth
                    into your sweaty cell
                    emission of culture

                    You go down
                    conversing
                    with ghost
                    children

III

I am the Kwakiutl youth
I pick strands of meat
like stringy figures
out of drunken mouth

                    You french me

anyway & the long fingers
of fishermen fondle
your slippery thighs

                    Come into my longhouse
                    all of mutèd light

You, yellow as cedar
salve & such purgatives
for longing in beer
stained hands

                             of a well … red man

        skin salmon pink
        as a fresh deposit
        slip, slightly dirty
        with chained pens
        & brunching bowls
        of faux pho, your
        talk of foreign
        food in Main St
        shops

                           This dance taken
with, from, by So much depends upon
a preposition in a solicitor's eye

Forbidden, policemen glisten
in nightsticked pines
                         Plum blossoms talk
        in the unspeakable accusative

Together, we shiver in the
shower, we embrace as the
shaman dictates on digital
media
        Hideoushystericalhalfnakedsavages
        we cling & mingle homosaps There
        is thirst in our thirst

                                      Chomp(wet) Chomp(wet)
                                    Chomp(wet) Chomp(wet)

IV

I am the Kwakiutl youth
impassive before a bear
my heart baits

I seek the dj

                   & (i)brow jd

speak
the unsound
          with baited breath
                 then whittle it
                          down

     vinyl grooves of midnight
     between reddening songs

I have reservations too Dogs bark
there Do they bark back to you
while drumskins redden in
British mouths like mine

               I awaken to a man
               in carny mirror I

     kick down the door
     & raid the place
     reading, writes
     in self/same
     tongue
          I bark at my great-grandfather
          & he lets me cuff him one
          & goes down
          looking down
          like Burt in *Deliverance*
          talking about the LAW

Blood omygodbloodmother, a strange
river of sticks & stones disturbed
in the dark where the constant stream
stilts the stream just where you're .
skinnydipping or paddling a smooth
white ass
               A stir of *wild* salmon

still invigorates
makes a case
of discarded
Kokanee
      among
spermatic
   stones

Maisie I re-enact your pretty death many nights
nights while the city while the Interior burns
while your sister becomes a stubborn river
dogs bark
about the gate while a V of raven SUVs
honks & speeds about the green
Leslie Hopper
turning green with mad hand signals over
his first dinner of oolichan grease oozing
like shattered oil tankers or rusty hulls
teeming with half-dead dehydra heads

REFRAIN:

I am the Kwakiutl youth
[Kwakwaka'wakw speaker
in the cornered, man from
Komuckway, Comox, "Place
of Plenty," "Abundance
Street," in social
dwelling grow-opted
out, a bachelor pad with
bookshelves from Sweden
& banquet tables from
Staples, but still so
famished, still hungry
on hardwood floor, still
a tad peckish]

I want to eat your
eyes first, then your
stomach full of haggis
or vindaloo or sushi
inside perogies, a
sure path to heart
or even arteries

in conversation
savour this heart
stuck in my throat
broken into 4
by these heirs

of long-fingered fisher
men with purse
seiners who
looked like
Tyrone Power
                    empowered with the mere
might of self-importance, assertion
language is, portaging across
global debris, past those
fishnets of celebrities
near extinction

                    yet telekinetic
                    with lottery
                    tickets

                              calling
                              out bingo
                              again &
                              again

Feast your eyes
upon my fetish

                    Naturally, there will be
                    masks & souvenirs in the
                    potlatch shop on your

                                   way out

As host, I apologize for being
impolite as a para/site Some
times, even before this feast
I want to eat my
        own words

                    & man they taste
                    like red heaven

                              Chomp(sky) Chomp(sky)
                              Chomp(sky) Chomp(sky)

B.C. Packers salmon seiner *BCP #45* was owned and operated by Harry Assu of Cape Mudge.

Image of Canadian five-dollar bill courtesy of the National Currency Collection, Currency Museum, Bank of Canada. Used and altered with the permission of the Bank of Canada.

BCP #45

        coasts through
              his long brown fingers
net–
   bitten
        That seiner
            has sailed
past
   how many sirens
           through how many
                banks

Give me five. Serial
numbered memory
of minted fish
slapping ...

      Changes
        hands

           Forty-nine
            years of wild
            fish may slip
             right through

your fingers

      But tomorrow
        morning, let me
           hold it up
         to the light

In House #5

I saw one of the best-
  combed minds of generations
talking in circles
only semi-senile
  doing close
    to ninety
      & sleek
        as a seal
          his mane
    slicked
back

        Quadra
      pebble
        in the
          palm

            *"Be a lawyer. We
            need more lawyers"*

                        Alzheimer's
                          or dementia
                        or plain
                          old age (the doctors
                            get confused)

    *"We marched to
    Victoria together
    for education for
    Indians …"*

μὴ   Don't
  κίνη   stir up
χέραδας   the stones

        *"Be a lawyer. We
        need more lawyers"*

Don't meddle
with a pebble

> *"They took my hand*
> *& welcomed me in*
>
> *They said*
> *   you speak"*

                  Do not
                    disturb
                  the stucco

Translations of Sappho flow in circles
in circles around the island along the
rather mistaken Discovery Passage
while great-uncle retells the same
   river more than once:

> *"Be a lawyer. I tell*
> *the young that. We*
> *need more lawyers"*

Ουτις. I am He-With-No-Name
Quite simply, I scratch burning
words with stick into sand &
learn to be the stick that comes
   alive & speaks coarsely within
      those lengthy atavistic fingers
                  while
                          finely
                combed
                    minds
                &
            the shamanic
       route of
         Ripple
         Roc k

        ex pl od es

"I remember a big carved wood frog displayed at
my father's potlatch that I really liked as a little
boy. The fun of seeing this frog is my first
memory in life ... [t]hat big frog was bought by
a collector from the stuff that was being taken
away from our people so they couldn't potlatch.
We want those things given back."
— Harry Assu (*Assu of Cape Mudge*, 46–47)

*Image courtesy of the National Museum of the
American Indian, Smithsonian Institution,
(11/5185). Photo: Photo Services.*

Wak'es

Ah, great *Lenape*, lend me your
tears for but one commercial
break
       giant *Menatay*
             kindling
                   Mahatuouh
    rocking *Mannahatta*
               of sad-eyed ladies
& Chelsea mornings
             most of all
Mahahachtanienk
        stumbling home
                 forgetful
of your cares
        & inherited memories
   you are
       almost listening
                Lenape:
    common people
    the real people
    riparian people

            We, the people
                 since 1794
have crossed the 49th
          perhaps faster
              & more frequently
than even
    literature
        & since I have heard
              of beefed-up
madness
    in that cattle-prodding
          process
             otherwise
known as
    homeland
       security

                              (to use the *Haudenosaunee*
                        term)
                                    & yes, I
               do
                     have an unflagged
                     book in my Eskimos
                     duffel bag
                                    carry-on!

I would love nothing
better than to observe
the grey Hudson billow
to unbutton my shirt
& play coy reading
play coy playing
a metaphysical
Whitmanesque
rough
          but Mannahatta
                              I have a
          frog
                     in my throat

Technically
               your throat
                                    my darling
               Why, my great-
          uncle would watch
it
stand
          upon a cradle
                              & hear it
whistling
          all by itself

But then a preacher man
came bustling in with fire
& brimstone & laid waste
to the peaceful islands of
the Kwa-Kutes, which
had hitherto fructified

with rivers of syrup
& put an end of their
feasts of elephant
tusks & unicorn
horn & taught
them women
were actually
rib-bits & stole
their sacred regalia
& took that singing
frog with a mission just
like that evil wizard in
Lord of the Rings, since
the frog was magical
& *whosoever cometh*
upon it yada yada
was written into
those glassy
eyes, etc

But then a character in the state
of York known as the Custodian
hulkishly tore open his tailored
shirt & rippled into his limo
& flung his chauffeur from
the roaring, nay soaring
vehicle, because he had
a inch of weirding, or
a wallop of feminine
intuition or whatall
you wanna call it
& it was swell &
all was swell
as he drove
across past
the sun
& landed
his wheels
more tanned than
Mink or Phaethon
& he bent the preacher

of men to his will, for
he had the gift of the
blab & what is more
the frog had sung to
him take me home
to great *Menatay*
& the preacher
was a smite slow
& his eyes were
full of masks &
coppers & lest
we forget, his
bigass mission
as the Custodian
veered back into
the cirrus clouds

Now
     I from the land
of
    This is my Village
              will remain
unbearingly
        polite & taciturn
only
    to tap you
           upon your fair
shoulder,
       Mannahatta
           to say the frog that bore
     witness is part
           of my family
&
  haunts my dreams
 like one of your
  incredibly
  tall sexual
thillboards
  the height
  of a Trojan
       horse

                    Can you not hear it
                                croaking …?

Deep
        in the financial
                        district
                            beneath a horizon-
                less horizon

    the frog
whistles
for a
Babel
of cabs
home-
ward
bound
with its
own
        finger-
                lickety
                    tongue
                                while upon
                                        a lily
                                            Basho weeps

        First we take Manhattan
                        then we take B.C.

Ahh … Mannahatta
                    I can't stay mad at you
            I love
                    your addictive friendliness
                    your multiplicity of hawkers
                    your streetwalking screens
                    your possibilities for opera
                    your provocative amnesia
even
        your teeming museums
                            This is only
                                    a trial

separation
        with a lingering
                custody
                      issue
                          since
one nippy
      night
          in 1922

                    Shhh … don't cry
                          Mannahatta
It won't be for long
        You can even
             keep
               your
                  Vermeers

    Just give me
    the frog & no
    one gets hurt

πάντα 'ρει

                    better
                            than be

                                        Rock
                            erodes

            breaks
                            down

                                                    better than
                                        be
                                Cedar
                stricken
                            mute
                                    & mossy
                                            & dead

better
        to be
                River
                        & better
                                run
                                    fast

Franz Boas posing for figure in USNM exhibit
entitled "Hamat'sa coming out of secret room."

*Negative MNH 8304, National Anthropological
Archives, Smithsonian Institution.*

Interpretative Dance
for Franz Boas

Listen
    (ethnographer of
                    bifurrrrrrrrrrrrrrcate tongue)
listen nicely
        & I will tell you
                a tale
so that you may know
                of me
                    & my particular line
        for a split-
second crawling
    through loop-
        hole in
                intellectual
            properties

Two hundred Indians are used for processing the salmon, and Chinese solder the
cans. It is quite interesting to watch the processing of the salmon. At the first table
women cut them open; at the next table heads and tails are removed. Then they are
drawn and thrown into
                a bath
                    where they are washed
                                then put into a machine
cuts them into seven parts
                and throws them into a
                            trough

    I will tell you of the first
                    place
                        where lived the Ligwilda'xw
in a village known as
                Tilted Ground
        where lived
                the old healer
                    & there is a myth

                                                        (do you know
                                                   what we did
                                                        not)
the one best equipped to guard
                                        the tree of life
must take the life of its present
guard
        & thereby become
                            its prisoner
                    until, until
the younger
healer
        turned seagreen
                        with envy

                                                                    to be
stuffed into cans. The lids are placed on top at another table and then in a soldering
machine which fastens the lids. They are then placed on a large iron
                                                        frame. soldering
is not checked in any way. The entire frame is then placed
                                                    into boiling water for
twenty minutes and then cooled. Finally the cans
                                        are packed
                                        into boxes

blindly threw
            sharpened bark
                            into salalberry bush
The next day, there was
                        nothing for it. Seagull eggs
were of less interest
                    than a length of kelp
                                        reaching to the
                                                    bottom
                                                        of the water
                The young
                        healer
                    shinnied
                                down
                    the kelp

Sister, do not despair. Look for me
every day along the beach. I ache to
explore the deepest part of the water

What began as a series of manual processes —

                                      fishboats were rowed; nets were hauled

by hand; cans were cut individually; workers on the line butchered

the fish one

                by one and stuffed the pieces into the tins — quickly became a

mechanized

 assembly line

               The steam retort, a large pressure cooker, replaced the ordinary kettles

               cooking the cans. Soldering machines replaced hand soldering, and the

               automatic can⁄making machine was introduced to mass produce the tins

       The young

healer

          made his

                   descent

& it took longer

than a very long

                 work day

                        until he was dancing upon the roof

                        of a house at the bottom of the water

                        Who the hell is rustling my roof-boards

                        is not an exact translation but close

       Inside, the healers could not heal the chief. Some-
body had wounded him with a sharpened bit of bark
when he was larking about in a salalberry bush, which
goes to show, stay away from nature if you can, yeah
but the young healer sidestepped the whole shame-
culture thing, thinking Richard Dawkins is right, part
of my urge to heal and give is to dominate, like birds
with their generosity with seeds, before post-Marxists
could get their mitts on what I know & usurp potlatch
theory for their own sad economic agenda, so in other
words it is my ancestral right, atavistically speaking, to
sing & flood the space with poems & stuff & maybe to

do a good turn here not only as a means of rectification
but as a means to gaining blood & glory in a showy way

Multi-bladed gang knives cut up several fish at once
into uniform sized pieces. Then, in 1906, the Smith
Butchering Machine was introduced.   Also

no one could see the sharpened bit of bark because the
chief was rather fat. Although in the interim since time
immemorial, First Nations' diet has changed. Education
abounds on the subject. Notwithstanding, four times the
young healer sucked mightily, claiming he was sucking out
all the sickness

known as the "Iron Chink" because it displaced
so many Chinese workers, it cleaned
        and butchered several   fish
at once, sixty to seventy-five

                    per minute

With sleight of hand, the
bit of sharpened bark was
removed
        & the chief had
        his appetite back

Young healer, I have clout
    with all the creatures of the sea
        now you will hold sway over all
            of Supernatural B.C.

                        (in those days
                        he would rather
                        have spat than
                        said Salish Sea)

The young healer
            yawned
                & figured
                    he better get going, since

he had a long climb
                    ahead of him

The fishery also mechanized. Gillnetters began adding small
                                        gas engines
        by 1913 more than eighty percent of the Fraser River fleet
                                            was motorized
        by the mid-1920s, gas engines became the norm north of Cape
                                        Caution

                    The next morning, he was not
                moving. Upon grey beach, his sister prodded
                his deadness with a stick. Hey, people grieve in
                different ways, eh. It was when she
                                        touched him

the canning industry
                    shifted from manual production
        to mechanized production, with resulting increases in
        productivity. The number of
                            plants
                                    fluctuated
                    from year
                            to year

                Alive! Sure beats the
                    alternative. The people
                                    in the village
        were pretty
                    impressed
                                except for
                                        that old
                                            healer
                who thought this magic
                was a trick, when it *was* a trick
                that had earned the young healer
                this magic

The cannery work
                    force lived close to the plants in neighbourhoods
racially segregated
                    as any big city ghetto. The Chinese occupied
"China houses"
                    wooden dormitories
                              provided by the company

        The way to test
                         his mettle
was to fake
            being sick –
                        that would sure
                                      fix
                that enchanted
                            braggart

                                sleeping, eating, gambling, playing, making
bootleg liquor, and tending to
                        pigs and chickens. Chinese workers used to make
                                                              kites
which they flew in their
                         spare time. As the years passed, Japanese
fishers joined Aboriginal boat crews, though the Japanese seldom
took
        inside jobs. They lived in
                            their own
                                    part of town

        The young healer
                         had more than a
                                        hunch
the old healer
                was feigning his complaint, in fact
        he *knew*
                for certain (same
                            way he knew
                                    just about
                                            everything)

Supervisors
                were always Euro-Canadians, who lived
in large houses
                    away from the clamour of the waterfront. The
result was a heady mixture of cultures and languages that was
every bit as
            "multicultural"
                        as Canada is today

so
    the young healer
                ripped out
                            the old
                    healer's
                            heart
                                liver
                                    intestines
                                            & lungs
            & yanked them
                        right out of
                            his ass

"What a motley crew
                you will find on one
of these British Columbia
                wharves!
                        What colouring
what a
        Babel of tongues —
                    Tlingits from Alaska, Haidas
            from the Queen Charlotte Islands, Tsimshians
            from the Skeena
                    Kwatiutls [sic]
                                from Vancouver, Chinamen
    Japanese, Greeks, Scandinavians, Englishmen and Yankees; men
    women, children, dogs, and from two to six
                                wooly bear cubs"

                    I was more
                            in the mood
                for a morality

play
       about pride
             before
                  a fall
one of those
       involving
             Raven
                & a comical
                       comeuppance

This is more like one of those early sagas
before the intervention of religious dogma
where stuff keeps happening, like in life
almost for no particular reason

               These
                  were almost
        the last words of
                the old healer
        before he noticed
               his internal
        lack of internals …

As for the
     young healer
             he had eliminated
the competition
       & was now footloose
             & fancy free
to heal
    (operating within
    stringent guidelines
   of the
       Kwakwaka'wakw
           health plan)
   & so he
      became a great
           healer
    taking the name
       K̲ate'na̲ts
   & becoming

the ancestor
of many people
who would
dance their dances
with ferocity
& sing their songs
with wild
brashness

& paint
everything
beyond überbrightness

until the day
beyond
tepid storytelling
&
trembling
voices
when our relations
will no longer
leave blanks
in our writings
I mean, for
things we do not
intuit
& that time
is gaining
on us
but I am afraid
that is another
story

500 Lines

I will not speak Kwak'wala.
I will not speak Kwak'wala.
I will not speak Kwak'wala.
I will not speak Kwak'wala.
I will not speak Kwak'wala.
I will not speak Kwak'wala.
I will not speak Kwak'wala.
I will not speak Kwak'wala.
I will not speak Kwak'wala.
I will not speak Kwak'wala.
I will not speak Kwak'wala.
I will not speak Kwak'wala.
I will not speak Kwak'wala.
I will not speak Kwak'wala.
I will not speak Kwak'wala.
I will not speak Kwak'wala.
I will not speak Kwak'wala.
I will not speak Kwak'wala.
I will not speak Kwak'wala.
I will not speak Kwak'wala.
I will not speak Kwak'wala.
I will not speak Kwak'wala.
I will not speak Kwak'wala.
I will not speak Kwak'wala.
I will not speak Kwak'wala.
I will not speak Kwak'wala.
I will not speak Kwak'wala.
I will not speak Kwak'wala.
I will not speak Kwak'wala.
I will not speak Kwak'wala.
I will not speak Kwak'wala.
I will not speak Kwak'wala.
I will not speak Kwak'wala.
I will not speak Kwak'wala.
I will not speak Kwak'wala.
I will not speak Kwak'wala.
I will not speak Kwak'wala.

I will not speak Kwak'wala.
I will not speak Kwak'wala.
I will not speak Kwak'wala.
I will not speak Kwak'wala.
I will not speak Kwak'wala.
I will not speak Kwak'wala.
I will not speak Kwak'wala.
I will not speak Kwak'wala.
I will not speak Kwak'wala.
I will not speak Kwak'wala.
I will not speak Kwak'wala.
I will not speak Kwak'wala.
I will not speak Kwak'wala.
I will not speak Kwak'wala.
I will not speak Kwak'wala.
I will not speak Kwak'wala.
I will not speak Kwak'wala.
I will not speak Kwak'wala.
I will not speak Kwak'wala.
I will not speak Kwak'wala.
I will not speak Kwak'wala.
I will not speak Kwak'wala.
I will not speak Kwak'wala.
I will not speak Kwak'wala.
I will not speak Kwak'wala.
I will not speak Kwak'wala.
I will not speak Kwak'wala.
I will not speak Kwak'wala.
I will not speak Kwak'wala.
I will not speak Kwak'wala.
I will not speak Kwak'wala.
I will not speak Kwak'wala.
I will not speak Kwak'wala.
I will not speak Kwak'wala.
I will not speak Kwak'wala.
I will not speak Kwak'wala.
I will not speak Kwak'wala.
I will not speak Kwak'wala.
I will not speak Kwak'wala.
I will not speak Kwak'wala.
I will not speak Kwak'wala.
I will not speak Kwak'wala.

I will not speak Kwak'wala.
I will not speak Kwak'wala.
I will not speak Kwak'wala.
I will not speak Kwak'wala.
I will not speak Kwak'wala.
I will not speak Kwak'wala.
I will not speak Kwak'wala.
I will not speak Kwak'wala.
I will not speak Kwak'wala.
I will not speak Kwak'wala.
I will not speak Kwak'wala.
I will not speak Kwak'wala.
I will not speak Kwak'wala.
I will not speak Kwak'wala.
I will not speak Kwak'wala.
I will not speak Kwak'wala.
I will not speak Kwak'wala.
I will not speak Kwak'wala.
I will not speak Kwak'wala.
I will not speak Kwak'wala.
I will not speak Kwak'wala.
I will not speak Kwak'wala.
I will not speak Kwak'wala.
I will not speak Kwak'wala.
I will not speak Kwak'wala.
I will not speak Kwak'wala.
I will not speak Kwak'wala.
I will not speak Kwak'wala.
I will not speak Kwak'wala.
I will not speak Kwak'wala.
I will not speak Kwak'wala.
I will not speak Kwak'wala.
I will not speak Kwak'wala.
I will not speak Kwak'wala.
I will not speak Kwak'wala.
I will not speak Kwak'wala.
I will not speak Kwak'wala.
I will not speak Kwak'wala.
I will not speak Kwak'wala.
I will not speak Kwak'wala.

I will not speak Kwak'wala.
I will not speak Kwak'wala.
I will not speak Kwak'wala.
I will not speak Kwak'wala.
I will not speak Kwak'wala.
I will not speak Kwak'wala.
I will not speak Kwak'wala.
I will not speak Kwak'wala.
I will not speak Kwak'wala.
I will not speak Kwak'wala.
I will not speak Kwak'wala.
I will not speak Kwak'wala.
I will not speak Kwak'wala.
I will not speak Kwak'wala.
I will not speak Kwak'wala.
I will not speak Kwak'wala.
I will not speak Kwak'wala.
I will not speak Kwak'wala.
I will not speak Kwak'wala.
I will not speak Kwak'wala.
I will not speak Kwak'wala.
I will not speak Kwak'wala.
I will not speak Kwak'wala.
I will not speak Kwak'wala.
I will not speak Kwak'wala.
I will not speak Kwak'wala.
I will not speak Kwak'wala.
I will not speak Kwak'wala.
I will not speak Kwak'wala.
I will not speak Kwak'wala.
I will not speak Kwak'wala.
I will not speak Kwak'wala.
I will not speak Kwak'wala.
I will not speak Kwak'wala.
I will not speak Kwak'wala.
I will not speak Kwak'wala.
I will not speak Kwak'wala.
I will not speak Kwak'wala.
I will not speak Kwak'wala.
I will not speak Kwak'wala.
I will not speak Kwak'wala.

I will not speak Kwak'wala.
I will not speak Kwak'wala.
I will not speak Kwak'wala.
I will not speak Kwak'wala.
I will not speak Kwak'wala.
I will not speak Kwak'wala.
I will not speak Kwak'wala.
I will not speak Kwak'wala.
I will not speak Kwak'wala.
I will not speak Kwak'wala.
I will not speak Kwak'wala.
I will not speak Kwak'wala.
I will not speak Kwak'wala.
I will not speak Kwak'wala.
I will not speak Kwak'wala.
I will not speak Kwak'wala.
I will not speak Kwak'wala.
I will not speak Kwak'wala.
I will not speak Kwak'wala.
I will not speak Kwak'wala.
I will not speak Kwak'wala.
I will not speak Kwak'wala.
I will not speak Kwak'wala.
I will not speak Kwak'wala.
I will not speak Kwak'wala.
I will not speak Kwak'wala.
I will not speak Kwak'wala.
I will not speak Kwak'wala.
I will not speak Kwak'wala.
I will not speak Kwak'wala.
I will not speak Kwak'wala.
I will not speak Kwak'wala.
I will not speak Kwak'wala.
I will not speak Kwak'wala.
I will not speak Kwak'wala.
I will not speak Kwak'wala.
I will not speak Kwak'wala.
I will not speak Kwak'wala.
I will not speak Kwak'wala.

I will not speak Kwak'wala.
I will not speak Kwak'wala.
I will not speak Kwak'wala.
I will not speak Kwak'wala.
I will not speak Kwak'wala.
I will not speak Kwak'wala.
I will not speak Kwak'wala.
I will not speak Kwak'wala.
I will not speak Kwak'wala.
I will not speak Kwak'wala.
I will not speak Kwak'wala.
I will not speak Kwak'wala.
I will not speak Kwak'wala.
I will not speak Kwak'wala.
I will not speak Kwak'wala.
I will not speak Kwak'wala.
I will not speak Kwak'wala.
I will not speak Kwak'wala.
I will not speak Kwak'wala.
I will not speak Kwak'wala.
I will not speak Kwak'wala.
I will not speak Kwak'wala.
I will not speak Kwak'wala.
I will not speak Kwak'wala.
I will not speak Kwak'wala.
I will not speak Kwak'wala.
I will not speak Kwak'wala.
I will not speak Kwak'wala.
I will not speak Kwak'wala.
I will not speak Kwak'wala.
I will not speak Kwak'wala.
I will not speak Kwak'wala.
I will not speak Kwak'wala.
I will not speak Kwak'wala.
I will not speak Kwak'wala.
I will not speak Kwak'wala.
I will not speak Kwak'wala.
I will not speak Kwak'wala.
I will not speak Kwak'wala.
I will not speak Kwak'wala.

I will not speak Kwak'wala.
I will not speak Kwak'wala.
I will not speak Kwak'wala.
I will not speak Kwak'wala.
I will not speak Kwak'wala.
I will not speak Kwak'wala.
I will not speak Kwak'wala.
I will not speak Kwak'wala.
I will not speak Kwak'wala.
I will not speak Kwak'wala.
I will not speak Kwak'wala.
I will not speak Kwak'wala.
I will not speak Kwak'wala.
I will not speak Kwak'wala.
I will not speak Kwak'wala.
I will not speak Kwak'wala.
I will not speak Kwak'wala.
I will not speak Kwak'wala.
I will not speak Kwak'wala.
I will not speak Kwak'wala.
I will not speak Kwak'wala.
I will not speak Kwak'wala.
I will not speak Kwak'wala.
I will not speak Kwak'wala.
I will not speak Kwak'wala.
I will not speak Kwak'wala.
I will not speak Kwak'wala.
I will not speak Kwak'wala.
I will not speak Kwak'wala.
I will not speak Kwak'wala.
I will not speak Kwak'wala.
I will not speak Kwak'wala.
I will not speak Kwak'wala.
I will not speak Kwak'wala.
I will not speak Kwak'wala.
I will not speak Kwak'wala.
I will not speak Kwak'wala.
I will not speak Kwak'wala.

I will not speak Kwak'wala.
I will not speak Kwak'wala.
I will not speak Kwak'wala.
I will not speak Kwak'wala.
I will not speak Kwak'wala.
I will not speak Kwak'wala.
I will not speak Kwak'wala.
I will not speak Kwak'wala.
I will not speak Kwak'wala.
I will not speak Kwak'wala.
I will not speak Kwak'wala.
I will not speak Kwak'wala.
I will not speak Kwak'wala.
I will not speak Kwak'wala.
I will not speak Kwak'wala.
I will not speak Kwak'wala.
I will not speak Kwak'wala.
I will not speak Kwak'wala.
I will not speak Kwak'wala.
I will not speak Kwak'wala.
I will not speak Kwak'wala.
I will not speak Kwak'wala.
I will not speak Kwak'wala.
I will not speak Kwak'wala.
I will not speak Kwak'wala.
I will not speak Kwak'wala.
I will not speak Kwak'wala.
I will not speak Kwak'wala.
I will not speak Kwak'wala.
I will not speak Kwak'wala.
I will not speak Kwak'wala.
I will not speak Kwak'wala.
I will not speak Kwak'wala.
I will not speak Kwak'wala.
I will not speak Kwak'wala.
I will not speak Kwak'wala.
I will not speak Kwak'wala.
I will not speak Kwak'wala.
I will not speak Kwak'wala.
I will not speak Kwak'wala.

I will not speak Kwak'wala.
I will not speak Kwak'wala.
I will not speak Kwak'wala.
I will not speak Kwak'wala.
I will not speak Kwak'wala.
I will not speak Kwak'wala.
I will not speak Kwak'wala.
I will not speak Kwak'wala.
I will not speak Kwak'wala.
I will not speak Kwak'wala.
I will not speak Kwak'wala.
I will not speak Kwak'wala.
I will not speak Kwak'wala.
I will not speak Kwak'wala.
I will not speak Kwak'wala.
I will not speak Kwak'wala.
I will not speak Kwak'wala.
I will not speak Kwak'wala.
I will not speak Kwak'wala.
I will not speak Kwak'wala.
I will not speak Kwak'wala.
I will not speak Kwak'wala.
I will not speak Kwak'wala.
I will not speak Kwak'wala.
I will not speak Kwak'wala.
I will not speak Kwak'wala.
I will not speak Kwak'wala.
I will not speak Kwak'wala.
I will not speak Kwak'wala.
I will not speak Kwak'wala.
I will not speak Kwak'wala.
I will not speak Kwak'wala.
I will not speak Kwak'wala.
I will not speak Kwak'wala.
I will not speak Kwak'wala.
I will not speak Kwak'wala.
I will not speak Kwak'wala.
I will not speak Kwak'wala.
I will not speak Kwak'wala.
I will not speak Kwak'wala.

I will not speak Kwak'wala.
I will not speak Kwak'wala.
I will not speak Kwak'wala.
I will not speak Kwak'wala.
I will not speak Kwak'wala.
I will not speak Kwak'wala.
I will not speak Kwak'wala.
I will not speak Kwak'wala.
I will not speak Kwak'wala.
I will not speak Kwak'wala.
I will not speak Kwak'wala.
I will not speak Kwak'wala.
I will not speak Kwak'wala.
I will not speak Kwak'wala.
I will not speak Kwak'wala.
I will not speak Kwak'wala.
I will not speak Kwak'wala.
I will not speak Kwak'wala.
I will not speak Kwak'wala.
I will not speak Kwak'wala.
I will not speak Kwak'wala.
I will not speak Kwak'wala.
I will not speak Kwak'wala.
I will not speak Kwak'wala.
I will not speak Kwak'wala.
I will not speak Kwak'wala.
I will not speak Kwak'wala.
I will not speak Kwak'wala.
I will not speak Kwak'wala.
I will not speak Kwak'wala.
I will not speak Kwak'wala.
I will not speak Kwak'wala.
I will not speak Kwak'wala.
I will not speak Kwak'wala.
I will not speak Kwak'wala.
I will not speak Kwak'wala.
I will not speak Kwak'wala.
I will not speak Kwak'wala.
I will not speak Kwak'wala.
I will not speak Kwak'wala.
I will not speak Kwak'wala.
I will not speak Kwak'wala.

I will not speak Kwak'wala.
I will not speak Kwak'wala.
I will not speak Kwak'wala.
I will not speak Kwak'wala.
I will not speak Kwak'wala.
I will not speak Kwak'wala.
I will not speak Kwak'wala.
I will not speak Kwak'wala.
I will not speak Kwak'wala.
I will not speak Kwak'wala.
I will not speak Kwak'wala.
I will not speak Kwak'wala.
I will not speak Kwak'wala.
I will not speak Kwak'wala.
I will not speak Kwak'wala.
I will not speak Kwak'wala.
I will not speak Kwak'wala.
I will not speak Kwak'wala.
I will not speak Kwak'wala.
I will not speak Kwak'wala.
I will not speak Kwak'wala.
I will not speak Kwak'wala.
I will not speak Kwak'wala.
I will not speak Kwak'wala.
I will not speak Kwak'wala.
I will not speak Kwak'wala.
I will not speak Kwak'wala.
I will not speak Kwak'wala.
I will not speak Kwak'wala.
I will not speak Kwak'wala.
I will not speak Kwak'wala.
I will not speak Kwak'wala.
I will not speak Kwak'wala.
I will not speak Kwak'wala.
I will not speak Kwak'wala.
I will not speak Kwak'wala.
I will not speak Kwak'wala.
I will not speak Kwak'wala.
I will not speak Kwak'wala.
I will not speak Kwak'wala.
I will not speak Kwak'wala.
I will not speak Kwak'wala.

I will not speak Kwak'wala.
I will not speak Kwak'wala.
I will not speak Kwak'wala.
I will not speak Kwak'wala.
I will not speak Kwak'wala.
I will not speak Kwak'wala.
I will not speak Kwak'wala.
I will not speak Kwak'wala.
I will not speak Kwak'wala.
I will not speak Kwak'wala.
I will not speak Kwak'wala.
I will not speak Kwak'wala.
I will not speak Kwak'wala.
I will not speak Kwak'wala.
I will not speak Kwak'wala.
I will not speak Kwak'wala.
I will not speak Kwak'wala.
I will not speak Kwak'wala.
I will not speak Kwak'wala.
I will not speak Kwak'wala.
I will not speak Kwak'wala.
I will not speak Kwak'wala.
I will not speak Kwak'wala.
I will not speak Kwak'wala.
I will not speak Kwak'wala.
I will not speak Kwak'wala.
I will not speak Kwak'wala.
I will not speak Kwak'wala.
I will not speak Kwak'wala.
I will not speak Kwak'wala.
I will not speak Kwak'wala.
I will not speak Kwak'wala.
I will not speak Kwak'wala.
I will not speak Kwak'wala.
I will not speak Kwak'wala.
I will not speak Kwak'wala.
I will not speak Kwak'wala.
I will not speak Kwak'wala.
I will not speak Kwak'wala.
I will not speak Kwak'wala.
I will not speak Kwak'wala.

Kwak'wala'mas?

K'i. K'isan kwak'wala.

Sources

Assu, Billy. *Indian Music of the Pacific Northwest Coast: Kwakiutl.* Collected and recorded by Ida Halpern. New York: Ethnic Folkways Library, 1981.

Assu, Harry. *Assu of Cape Mudge: Recollections of a Coastal Indian Chief.* Vancouver: UBC Press, 1989.

Boas, Franz. *Indian Myths & Legends from the North Pacific Coast of America.* Edited and annotated by Randy Bouchard and Dorothy Kennedy. Vancouver: Talonbooks, 2006.

Bowering, George. *The Gangs of Kosmos.* Toronto: House of Anansi, 1969.

Bracken, Christopher. *The Potlatch Papers: A Colonial Case History.* Chicago: The University of Chicago Press, 1997.

Clements, Marie and Rita Leistner. *The Edward Curtis Project: A Modern Picture Story.* Vancouver: Talonbooks, 2010.

Jensen, Doreen and Polly Sargent. *Robes of Power: Totem Poles on Cloth.* Vancouver: UBC Press, 1986.

Lévi-Strauss, Claude. *The Way of the Masks.* Seattle: University of Washington Press, 1988.

Marlatt, Daphne. *Selected Writing: Net Work.* Vancouver: Talonbooks, 1980.

_____. *Vancouver poems.* Toronto: Coach House Press, 1972.

Sewid, James. *Guests Never Leave Hungry: The Autobiography of James Sewid, a Kwakiutl Indian.* Edited by James P. Spradley. New Haven and London: Yale University Press, 1969.

Sewid-Smith, Daisy: *Prosecution or Persecution.* Cape Mudge: Nu-yum-balees Society, 1979.

Stewart, Hilary. *Looking at Indian Art of the Northwest Coast.* Washington: University of Washington Press, 1979.

Wallas, James. *Kwakiutl Legends.* Surrey, B.C. and Blaine, WA.: Hancock House Publishing, 1989.

Acknowledgements

I would like to thank Daphne Marlatt, Roy Miki, and Karl Siegler for their continual encouragement, support, and friendship. Their ongoing interest in my writing and this book in particular never ceases to do me the finest honour I could ever hope to receive.

I would also like to thank Kevin Williams, Vicki Williams, and Gregory Gibson for all their tireless efforts on my behalf.

I would like to thank Rita Wong and Russell Wallace for their confidence in my work and their belief in this project.

I would like to thank the Canada Arts Council and the BC Arts Council for their assistance and support of a project and writings concerning First Nations' and Kwakwaka'wakw culture in British Columbia.

This heartfelt gratitude extends to Alison J. Dodd and Catherine Gilbert for contributing their astonishing photographs from Quadra Island for this project.

I would like to thank my great-grandfather Chief Billy Assu, my great-uncle Chief Harry Assu, and my relation Chief James Sewid for displaying leadership in many issues concerning Native education and for their efforts to document fragments of time immemorial in order that they may survive in times ahead.

Most of all, I would like to thank my mother for inspiring me with her stories and examples of Kwakwaka'wakw life and what it is like to live in the city and yet live one's life at sea.